HOW TO GUIDE
GIRL SCOUT BROWNIES ON

BROWNIE QUEST

IT'S YOUR WORLD—CHANGE IT! *A LEADERSHIP JOURNEY*

Girl Scouts of the USA

CHAIR, NATIONAL BOARD OF DIRECTORS	CHIEF EXECUTIVE OFFICER	EXECUTIVE VICE PRESIDENT, MISSION TO MARKET	VICE PRESIDENT, PROGRAM DEVELOPMENT
Patricia Diaz Dennis	Kathy Cloninger	Norma I. Barquet	Eileen Doyle

BROWNIE WRITING TEAM: Ann Redpath, Laura Tuchman

CONTRIBUTORS: Tia Disick, Kate Gottlieb, Toi James, Maja Ninkovic, Monica Shah, María L. Cabán

ILLUSTRATED BY Helena Garcia

DESIGNED BY Parham Santana

© 2008 by Girl Scouts of the USA

First published in 2008 by Girl Scouts of the USA
420 Fifth Avenue, New York, NY 10018-2798
www.girlscouts.org

ISBN: 978-0-88441-712-5

Printed in Italy

1 2 3 4 5 6 7 8 9/ 16 15 14 13 12 11 10 09 08

Page 20: Photo by Debra Sprague, Dhahran, Saudi Arabia.

CONTENTS

"Brownies are game for everything and anything. I like it when they get in their ring and take a vote and learn what it means to make decisions and be listened to— you can witness their first moment of empowerment."

— Julie Brown, Girl Scout volunteer, Middleburg, Florida

LET THE QUEST BEGIN!

Shhhhh! You are about to guide a group of Girl Scout Brownies on a quest to find three very important keys. From the start, you'll know exactly what these keys are. But the girls won't have a clue. This is a quest, after all! So it's important to keep the fun and mystery going. Play it up so the Brownies can uncover the meaning of the keys as they go.

As second- and third-graders, Girl Scout Brownies are old enough to begin to understand and appreciate the concept and value of leadership. The three keys they will uncover along this journey are the keys of the Girl Scout leadership philosophy—Discover, Connect, and Take Action.

To find each key, Brownies will take three steps. A step might be a game, a brainstorming session, or an activity that calls for the Brownies to connect with their family or community. The Quest Master Map provided in this guide offers you and the girls a way to track your progress through the Quest. Details of each step are given on the awards page (8), in the Snapshot of the Quest (pages 10-11), and in the sample sessions. Just don't give away the details to the Brownies!

You may be wondering: What if some girls uncover the meaning of the keys before others? Stay mum and keep the suspense going as best you can. Say something like, "Hmm, what gave you that idea?" Or try steering the conversation a bit with a question like, "*What else do you think this key might be?*"

Working with the Girls' Brownie Quest Book

FOR FUN AND MEMORIES

Don't feel you need to give the Brownies "homework" to fill in all the pages of their Quest book. The activities are for girls who want to continue the fun and thinking between Team meetings. You'll find it helpful, though, to encourage each Brownie to have her own Quest book on hand at each session. It's something she and her family will look back on as a rich keepsake of her Girl Scout Brownie experience.

The girls' book is divided into two trails, the Trail of the ELF Adventure and the Trail of the Three Keys. The first trail features "The ELF Adventure," a story of three Brownie friends, their encounter with an elf, and their effort to save a family of trees. Each chapter of the story is accompanied by activities the girls can enjoy on their own or with friends and family. Encourage the girls to explore this trail whenever they like.

The Trail of the Three Keys is the trail you and the girls will follow whenever you gather. In the girls' book, this trail also offers activities and stories, and has space for adding mementos and jotting down reflections and ideas.

A Brownie Story and a Helpful Elf

In the story "The ELF Adventure," three fictional friends (Campbell, Jamila, and Alejandra), their families, and the community of Green Falls all deepen the Brownies' understanding of Girl Scouting as a global sisterhood of girls and women who are improving the world. Along the Quest, the Brownies also explore stories of real girls taking action around the globe.

The Brownie tree house makes the idea of belonging to this global network real and tangible to the girls. The idea of a Brownie Team is used, too, mostly to emphasize how the Girl Scout Brownies cooperate along the Quest. After Chapter 1 of "The ELF Adventure," for example, the girls' book features a "Friendship Game" with questions to answer and activities to try with friends. These are options that the girls can enjoy on their own or with you and their full Brownie Team.

Two other "friends"—Juliette Gordon Low and a fictional elf—are also important to the Quest. The Brownies uncover how Low, the founder of the Girl Scout Movement, discovered, connected, and took action as an early-20th-century leader. As for the elf, Girl Scout Brownie stories have always featured a magical elf with one very big job: making girls see that they are capable of remarkable things, especially if they work together. The tradition of the Brownie elf dates back to old English tales of Brownies who literally *were* elves: tiny creatures who did good deeds and helpful work. (The name "Brownies" was first given to the little sisters of Girl Guides in 1915, by Lord Robert Baden-Powell, the founder of Scouting.)

Throughout the Quest, an elf continues to play the historic helper role as the real Brownies move forward to uncover a whole new meaning for "ELF": Explore, Link Arms, and Fly into Action.

Awards Along the Quest

LET THE MASTER MAP PLAY UP THE SEARCH

You'll find it useful to use your Quest Master Map in every session of the Quest—to play up the idea that every time you and the Brownies get together, you're on a search.

Here's a handy guide to the nine steps the Brownies will take to find—and earn—the keys to leadership (all the steps are built into the session plans, too):

To find the **Discover Key**, *Brownies discover:*

- **their special qualities and talents**
- **the values of the Girl Scout Law**
- **the special qualities and values of their families**

To find the **Connect Key**, *Brownies connect:*

- **as a Brownie Team**
- **with their families on a healthy-living activity**
- **with their communities to increase healthy-living opportunities**

To find the **Take Action Key**, *Brownies:*

- **identify a community place where they can Take Action**
- **plan to Take Action**
- **improve their world by carrying out their Take Action Project**

As Brownies move through these nine steps, the Quest Master Map offers a visual record of their progress along the Quest. The girls have their own mini version of the Quest Map in their book.

At the end of the Quest, the girls also earn the journey's culminating award—the **Brownie Quest Award**. This is the master lock that needs all three of their keys in order to open. Through this award, the Brownies come to see that, together, their three keys—Discover, Connect, and Take Action—unlock the meaning of leadership.

WHAT IF A GIRL MISSES AN AWARD STEP?

Find a way for her to do something similar to what she missed so she can still earn the award with her Team. If she misses the day that the Team heads home to take part in a family activity, she can do the activity after a later session and still share her results with the Team. (And if a girl forgets to bring back an activity, or her family hasn't had a chance to do it with her, she can do it at a later time; or you can help her think of some other ways to accomplish something similar.) If a girl misses the Brownie Brainstorm or Brownie Team Trade, she can still offer up her own ideas to the Team. If she misses some Take Action time, she can take the lead in a follow-up step, such as talking with the other members and sharing what they learned.

When girls miss a meeting, your goal is to assist them in finding ways to have the same learning and growing opportunity—and to understand how they can contribute to the Team. Girls may not have the exact same experience but they can each take away new insights, connections, and a sense of accomplishment. As you guide girls through meaningful challenges, you might call on the full Team of Brownies to brainstorm together about how girls who miss some steps can best get back on track with the journey.

Snapshot of the Quest

SESSION 1

Discovering ...

- **You:** Brownies join in a circle and, with a ball toss, introduce themselves and name their skills and qualities.
- **Values:** Brownies "go ELF" to search for values of the Girl Scout Law.
- **Family:** Each Brownie heads home to discover her family's special qualities and the value of the Law that resonates most with her family.

SESSION 2

Discovering and Connecting ...

- **In the Brownie Star Circle:** Brownies share their family discoveries and join in the first Quest ceremony, earning their first key.
- **By Teaming Up:** Brownies play cooperative games, then create their own Team Agreement.
- **With Family:** Brownies commit to leading a healthy-living activity with their families.

SESSION 3

Connecting and Taking Action ...

- **Making a Circle Map:** Brownies explore how the "circles" of their lives grow outward: Me, Family, Girl Scouts, Community, World.
- **Posting Commitments:** In the map's Family circle, Brownies post Commitment Cards noting their family's healthy-living actions.
- **Caring for Community:** The Team expands its circle of caring through two stories—one real, one fictional—that serve as springboards to writing letters to a school or town official to seek a healthy-living improvement.
- **Earning the Second Key:** Brownies close with the Quest's second award ceremony.

SESSION 4

Choosing a Take Action Project

- **Brownie Brainstorm:** Team members consider community places where they could Take Action to make a difference.
- **Brownie Team Trade:** The Team "goes ELF" while deciding on top ideas for taking action.
- **Brownie Plan:** The Team talks about preparations and materials they need to Take Action.

SESSIONS 5 & 6	**Taking Action and Making the World a Better Place**
	Depending on the Brownies' Take Action Project, these two sessions may overlap or combine so that you and the girls can select those activities that best fit your project schedule.

SESSION 5

Taking Action

- **Brownies Get Busy:** Depending on their project, the Team creates a skit, gathers supplies or donations, learns about a community issue, etc.
- **Brownie Team Reflects:** The girls describe their project and their thoughts about it.
- **ELFing It Up:** Time permitting, the Team creates "what if?" endings to "The ELF Adventure" story, sings Brownie songs, or makes a gift to swap.

SESSION 6

Making the World a Better Place

- **Wrapping Up:** Brownies conclude their efforts to reach out and make an impact in their community.
- **ELFing It Up One More Time:** Time permitting, the Team explores new endings/adventures for "The ELF Adventure," makes healthy treats, tries the extra puzzles and activities in their Quest books, or creates a closing ceremony.
- **Meeting Juliette:** The Team considers how Juliette Gordon Low discovered, connected, and took action, and adds a note to her in their books.
- **Earning the Third Key:** Brownies take part in their third award ceremony.

SESSION 7

Unlocking the Code to Leadership: Celebration and Reflection

(This celebration can take place at the end of Session 6 or be a separate Session 7 "event" with family and friends.)

- **Unlocking the Leadership Code:** Putting their keys together, Brownies find that when they Discover, Connect, and Take Action, they are leaders. They earn the Quest Award and add a "leadership commitment" card to their Quest books.
- **Cheers and a Big Send-Off:** The Team carries out its closing ceremony, reciting the Girl Scout Promise and Law, and sharing songs, memories, and stories of the Quest.

Use the Brownie
Family and Friends
Network forms starting
on the next page as
a handy way to make
everyone aware of
the Brownie Team's
activities. The forms,
which are meant to
be photocopied (they
can be found online at
www.girlscouts.org),
even note when the
Brownies have a little
"take home" project to
do with their families.
If you prefer, you can
always reach out to the
Brownies' families and
friends in less formal
ways—e-mail, phone,
in-person chats.

Getting Support: The Brownie Family and Friends Network

You'll get a break *and* expand the girls' awareness of community by asking the family members, friends, and even friends of friends to visit the Brownie Team. So go ahead and "hand off" activities and prep steps to the Brownie Family and Friends Network. And keep in mind, Brownies aspire up. They will love to hear from and spend time with older girls as they progress along the Quest. Here are a few suggestions for cultivating the network:

• Before the Quest begins, see if you can have a brief get-together (even online!) with parents, caregivers, relatives, and friends. Find out who likes to do what, identify assistants for various activities along the Quest, and see who has time for behind-the-scenes preparations, gathering supplies (pads, markers, glitter, glue), or "smart snack" duty. Keep in mind that, in some families, an aunt, older sibling, cousin, grandparent, or other adult may be most able to participate. (See the Brownie Family and Friends Network Sign-Up Form, page 16).

• Ask your Girl Scout council to identify a Girl Scout Cadette (or two!) to join the Quest. By following the steps on the Girl Scout Cadette LiA Award form (page 17-19), Cadette assistants will enjoy earning an award for their leadership as they support the Brownies on their Quest.

• As part of the Quest, the Brownie Team will choose ideas for its own Take Action Project. Although it is important not to plan the project *for* the Brownies, you'll find it helpful to identify possible contacts in the community ahead of time. Then, once the Brownie Team makes a decision, you'll have a head start on who might be able to assist in planning the specifics.

Welcome!

Dear Brownie Friends and Family Network:

Your Brownie is on a Quest—a special journey to find out what it means to be a leader. This experience will benefit her by guiding her to understand her own skills and values as she teams with others, learns to identify community needs, and then acts to better her community, inspiring others along the way.

On the Quest, your Brownie will earn three keys and then solve the mystery of what they open!

Throughout their journey, your Brownie and her Brownie Team will need a little assistance from the Brownie Family and Friends Network! Talking to your Brownie between each session of the Quest will make the experience even more beneficial to her! Just use the information provided on the attached overview to follow her experiences on the Quest.

You will notice that after a few of the sessions, your Brownie will bring home a "Brownie Family Activity." After assisting your Brownie with the activity, be sure to send it back with her to the next session. Each activity on the Brownie Quest builds into the next one.

Later in the Quest the Brownies will team up on a project to help their community. After the girls decide what kind of project to do, we'll need help with transportation and supplies. Stay tuned for more information!

Sincerely,

_____

Brownie Quest Guide

Contact Info

Phone _____

E-mail _____

Girl Scout Council (name and phone number) _____

Girl Scout Brownie Quest

Overview

for the Brownie Friends and Family Network

_____

Date   Place   Time

The girls will discover the talents and qualities that make them unique. They will also discover the values of the Girl Scout Law.

After the session, look at pages 49-51 of the Brownie Quest book with your Brownie. Assist her in discovering the talents, qualities, and values your family is proud of by completing the "Discovering Family" activity she will bring home.

Session 2: Discovering and Connecting

_____

Date   Place   Time

The girls will earn the first key—so be sure they return their "Discovering Family" stars.

Then the girls will practice working together as a Team—and create a Team Agreement. Each Brownie will come home with a "Connect" project to show her family members she cares about them. Take a little time during the week to do the project together.

Session 3: Connecting and Taking Action

_____

Date   Place   Time

The Brownies will share ideas about how they connected with their families on a new healthy-living habit, so be sure your Brownie returns her Commitment Card. The Brownies will then explore how the circles of their lives grow out—from "me" to "family" to "Girl Scouts" to the "community" to the whole world. They will practice being active members of their community by teaming up and writing a simple letter to someone in their community about something they care about. And before the session ends, they will have earned the second key! Ask them about it when they come home!

Session 4: Choosing a Take Action Project

_____

Date   Place   Time

The girls will take part in a Brownie Brainstorm to think about all the places and people in the community who might need their help. Then they'll learn to make a decision—as part of a Team—and choose some ideas so they can Fly into Action and make a difference in the community.

Stay tuned for news about what the Brownie Team will do during Sessions 5 and 6. We may need help with:

• Transportation

• Supplies

• Contacts in the community

Session 5: Taking Action
During this time, the Brownies will be doing their community action project. Let us know if you can assist!

Session 6: Making the World a Better Place

The Brownies will be finishing their Take Action Project and earning their third key. Stay tuned for more information about the place and time of the session.

Session 7: Closing Celebration

When the Brownies complete the Quest, they will have a celebration as they earn their Brownie Quest Award and unlock its mystery by using their three keys. They'll also have a chance to talk about everything they have accomplished on the Quest. Let us know if you can help us plan the party.

_____

Date   Place   Time

Girl Scout Brownie Quest

Family and Friends Network

Sign-Up Form

The Brownie Team needs help. Can anyone in your family or your circle of connections provide these kinds of support?

I or someone I know can assist with:

_____ Transportation

_____ Smart snacks

_____ Community action

_____ Celebration

_____ Day trip

_____ Some of the meetings

Name _____

My Brownie's name _____

Phone _____

E-mail _____

Dear Girl Scout Cadette,

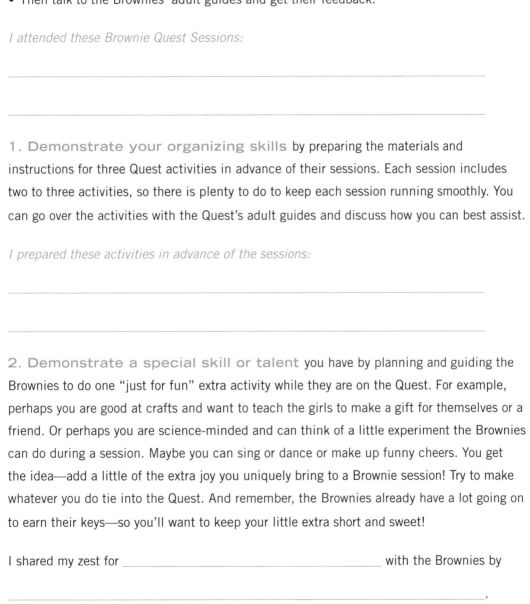

Here's your chance to show your leadership skills as you assist your Brownie sisters along their special quest! To earn your LiA (Leader in Action) Award for the Brownie Quest:

- Demonstrate your commitment by actively assisting during four sessions of the Brownie Quest (even better, come to all of them!).
- Do Steps 1–3 as outlined on these pages.
- Reflect on your experience using the questions on these pages.
- Then talk to the Brownies' adult guides and get their feedback.

I attended these Brownie Quest Sessions:

_____

_____

1. Demonstrate your organizing skills by preparing the materials and instructions for three Quest activities in advance of their sessions. Each session includes two to three activities, so there is plenty to do to keep each session running smoothly. You can go over the activities with the Quest's adult guides and discuss how you can best assist.

I prepared these activities in advance of the sessions:

_____

_____

2. Demonstrate a special skill or talent you have by planning and guiding the Brownies to do one "just for fun" extra activity while they are on the Quest. For example, perhaps you are good at crafts and want to teach the girls to make a gift for themselves or a friend. Or perhaps you are science-minded and can think of a little experiment the Brownies can do during a session. Maybe you can sing or dance or make up funny cheers. You get the idea—add a little of the extra joy you uniquely bring to a Brownie session! Try to make whatever you do tie into the Quest. And remember, the Brownies already have a lot going on to earn their keys—so you'll want to keep your little extra short and sweet!

I shared my zest for _____ with the Brownies by

_____ .

3. While on the Quest, the Brownies will be leading their families and communities in "healthy-living" actions like making and enjoying healthy treats or playing a game that gets people up and moving. Take the healthy living even further by doing one of these:

- Bring the fixings for a simple, healthy snack to a session (carrots and low-fat dip; apples and yogurt), assist the girls in "making" the treat, and explain (perhaps on poster board)—in a Brownie-friendly way—why that snack is better then something else (like _____).

- Teach the Brownies how to do a simple exercise or stretch that you know and like, and use it as a "quick break" between activities. Offer a short explanation of why it's good!

- Bring some music and get everybody moving as the meeting starts or ends—or when an energy boost is needed! Offer a quick explanation of why it's good!

While on the Quest, the Brownies will be Discovering, Connecting, and Taking Action (shhh . . . don't tell them those are the names of the keys they are finding!). Think about how you are Discovering, Connecting, and Taking Action along with them . . . and take a little time to reflect on your experience. Think about what you've learned and then answer these questions:

I discovered that a value that really matters to me is:

_____

_____

I discovered that a special skill or quality I enjoy using with others is:

_____

_____

I find it challenging to "connect" with younger girls because they

_____

_____

I enjoy connecting with the adults involved with the Quest because

_____

_____

When the Brownies were choosing and doing their Take Action Project I felt
_____ *because* _____

I am glad I took action to assist in leading the Brownie Quest because

_____

_____

Talk to the adults guiding the Quest. Find out one thing you did during the Brownie Quest that was really, really great (a perfect 10!). Then find out one thing that you can keep in mind—to practice for the next time you team up with younger girls in Girl Scouts.

One thing I did that was a perfect 10:

_____

_____

One thing I will keep practicing:

_____

_____

Congratulations! You have shown that you are a true leader!

"**What I like best** about Brownies
is the creativity they have."

—Jennifer M. Wiseman, Girl Scout volunteer, Winchester, Virginia

YOU AND YOUR GROUP OF BROWNIES

Throughout this journey, you and the girls will gain deeper knowledge of one another and the rich traditions of Girl Scouting. So take some time to understand the likes and needs of Brownie-age girls, and then dip into the history of Girl Scouts and the "what and how" of creating quality Girl Scout experiences.

As you read about the long-lasting leadership benefits of Girl Scouting, think about your own perspective on leadership. Your interest and enthusiasm are sure to be a driving force for the Brownies as they travel along the Quest.

Understanding Brownie-Age Girls

Your second- and third-grade companions on the Brownie Quest are going to call upon you to understand who they are at this stage of their development. Here are a few quick tips:

Second-graders . . .

Like doing things their own way.

So be sure to give them extra attention when they are working in groups.

Need routine, structure, and predictability.

So try keeping certain elements of meetings consistent—such as always having openings and closings.

Want to be able to finish things they start.

So be patient if things take longer than you would have thought.

Third-graders . . .

Like to do things in groups.

So be sure to give them lots of chances to team up.

Need help focusing their energy and enthusiasm.

So try giving them clear and specific directions.

Want lots of encouragement.

So try re-directing them if they get frustrated.

In a mixed group of second- and third-graders, you'll find it helpful to:

Ask the older girls to help and/or mentor the younger ones.

Provide lots of opportunities for active play—if you can take it outdoors, all the better!

Give plenty of praise and encouragement to help them through any challenges.

Provide them with some time in special "second-grade" and "third-grade" mini-teams.

What + How: Creating a Quality Experience

It's not just *what* girls do, but *how* you engage them that creates a high-quality experience. All Girl Scout activities are built on three processes—Girl Led, Cooperative Learning, and Learning by Doing—that make Girl Scouting unique from school and other extracurricular activities. When used together, these processes ensure the quality and promote the fun and friendship so integral to Girl Scouting. Take some time to understand these processes and how to use them with Girl Scout Brownies.

Girl Led

"Girl Led" is just what it sounds like—girls play an active part in figuring out the what, where, when, how, and why of their activities. So encourage them to lead the planning, decision-making, learning, and fun as much as possible. This ensures that girls are engaged in their learning and experience leadership opportunities as they prepare to become active participants in their local and global communities. With Brownies, this might mean:

• Brainstorming lists of possibilities

• Letting them select from some choices (for opening and closing ceremonies, for example)

• Selecting "add-ons" for the Quest (crafts, trips, etc.)

• Allowing the girls to learn from plans that don't go quite right (as long as everyone is safe!). They can talk about what they'd do differently next time.

Some girl-led experiences are built into Quest sessions to make it easy for you. For example, during Session 4, the Brownie Brainstorm has the girls identifying and beginning to plan a Take Action Project.

Learning by Doing

Learning by Doing, also known as Experiential Learning, is a hands-on learning process that engages girls in continuous cycles of action and reflection that result in deeper understanding of concepts and mastery of practical skills. As they participate in meaningful activities and then reflect on them, girls get to explore their own questions, discover answers, gain new skills, and share ideas and observations with others. Throughout the process, it's important for girls to be able to connect their experiences to their lives and apply what they have learned to their future experiences.

For the Brownie Team, this means giving the girls (and yourself!) some quiet time along the Quest to stop, think, talk, and reflect. Resist the urge to rush from "doing" to "more doing," and try to follow the discussion tips and questions provided to assist the Brownies in getting deeper meaning from what they have just done. Plenty of additional tips are woven into this guide, and the girls have even more opportunities to reflect and apply their experiences through the optional exercises in their Quest books.

Cooperative Learning

Through cooperative learning, girls work together toward shared goals in an atmosphere of respect and collaboration that encourages the sharing of skills, knowledge, and learning. Working together in all-girl environments also encourages girls to feel powerful and emotionally and physically safe, and it allows them to experience a sense of belonging even in the most diverse groups. With Brownies, you can try:

• Providing plenty of opportunities for teaming up in mini-groups

• Making decisions together as a Team (even about small things like what snack to serve at the next session)

• Giving the girls a minute or two to work out conflicts before you jump in (as long as physical safety isn't an issue)

Cooperative learning experiences are also built into the Quest. For example, during Session 2, the Brownies engage in Team play and then use the experience to create their own Team Agreement. At future sessions, you can display the agreement and ask the girls to reflect on their efforts to stick to it.

Girl Scout Traditions and Ceremonies

Celebrating Girl Scout traditions connects girls to one another, to their sister Girl Scouts and Girl Guides around the world, and to the generations of girls who were Girl Scouts before them.

Along the Quest, you'll notice frequent opportunities to create a Brownie Circle—for Team reflections and ceremonies. This simple tradition sets the Brownie Quest apart from any other activity girls this age will likely do. It marks the time and experience as special—the Quest is a big event in the lives of young girls!

A few other Girl Scout traditions are mentioned here (your local Girl Scout council will have many more). Try incorporating some into your Quest sessions—they will really help the girls understand that they're part of a sisterhood of leaders. And don't forget to involve them in creating some new traditions—even a few silly songs!

Girl Scout Sign

The Girl Scout sign is made when you say the Girl Scout Promise. The sign is formed with the right hand, by using the thumb to hold down the little finger, leaving the three middle fingers extended (these three fingers represent the three parts of the Promise).

Girl Scout Handshake

HOW TO
GIRL SCOUT HANDSHAKE

The Girl Scout handshake is the way many Girl Guides and Girl Scouts greet each other. They shake their left hands while making the Girl Scout sign with their right hand. The left-handed handshake represents friendship because the left hand is closer to the heart than the right.

Friendship Circle

The Friendship Circle is often formed at the end of meetings or campfires as a sort of closing ceremony. Everyone gathers in a circle, and each girl crosses her right arm over her left and holds hands with the person on each side. Once everyone is silent, the leader starts the friendship squeeze by squeezing the hand of the person next to her. One by one, each girl passes on the squeeze until it travels around the full circle.

Ceremonies and the Power of Belonging

Ceremonies have always been part of the fun of being a Girl Scout. When girls gather in a ceremony, they share their collective strengths, hopes, and accomplishments and experience the power of belonging.

The Brownies may not be able to fully understand the sense of oneness achieved by coming together in a ceremony, but they do understand that a ceremony is special and they enjoy the sense of dignity ceremonies convey. When Brownies gather together, they are up to important stuff!

Ceremonies for Brownies can be simple and short, and they're best when they are carried out in a happy and spontaneous mood. So try not to make them feel like a "must-do" at Brownie gatherings.

Along the Quest, Brownies have chants and cheers and ceremonies for finding their keys. You can create more opportunities for simple ceremonies along the way. You might make a ceremony out of sitting in a circle together to read the episodes of "The ELF Adventure" or ask the girls to partner with you to create an energizing way to start your time together.

Ceremonies may involve singing, pantomiming, saying memorized lines, or expressing a spontaneous thought or feeling. A ceremony can be as simple as choosing a line from the Girl Scout Law and inviting each Brownie to say what it means to her.

You may also like to try some ideas culled from the rich history of ceremony in Girl Scouting. Feel free to adapt them as you gather with the Brownies and guide them to express feelings of happiness, gratitude, respect, praise, or accomplishment along the Quest.

Ceremonies from the Girl Scout Archives
For Opening a Meeting

Fairy or Dancing Ring: The girls dance or skip into a circle formation to music, or a drum, or a song sung by the girls. Then they dance or skip while singing a Brownie song (see page 67 of the girls' book).

Surprise: This ceremony is almost too simple to describe but is fun for children. The adult must plan to keep her back toward the door during the opening minutes of the meeting. Each girl, on arrival, tiptoes in to the side of the leader, calling "surprise" when she gets there.

MAKE YOUR OWN TRADITIONS

As you and the Brownies come up with enjoyable ways to open or close your time together, by all means repeat them. With repetition, ceremonies become cherished traditions.

28

For Closing a Meeting

Cleanup: The children skip about the room (or fly into action), picking up materials and arranging things neatly. All the while they're singing (to the tune of "London Bridge"):

Weave the magic in and out, in and out, in and out,
Weave the magic in and out, we are Brownies!
We have tidied everything, everything, everything,
We have tidied everything, we are Brownies!

Then the Brownies gather before the adult volunteer, who asks:
Is everything finished?

The girls answer: *Everything.*

The adult volunteer asks: *Is nothing left?*

The girls answer: *Nothing!*

The adult volunteer says: *Then be gone!*

Magic Tunnel: When hats and coats are on, the Brownies stand in two lines, making arches with their arms. The two farthest from the door go under the arches, then the next two, and so on, so that the tunnel diminishes and the last two go out under the arms of their adult guides.

Slip Away Silently: In a closing ring, the Brownies sing a favorite good-night song, followed by silence. The leader then says, "Slip away," and every child quickly and quietly slips out to her waiting parents.

Health, Safety, and Well-Being

The emotional and physical safety and well-being of girls is of paramount importance in Girl Scouting. Look out for the safety of girls by following *Safety-Wise* when planning all gatherings and trips, and:

- Checking into any additional safety guidelines your Girl Scout council might have, based on local issues

- Talking to girls and their families about special needs or concerns

Welcoming Girls with Disabilities

Girl Scouting embraces girls with many different needs at all age levels and is guided by a very specific and positive philosophy of inclusion that benefits all: Each girl is an equal and valued member of a group with typically developing peers.

As an adult volunteer, you have the chance to improve the way society views girls with disabilities. One way to start is with language. Your words have a huge impact on the process of inclusion. People-First Language puts the person before the disability:

CONTACT INFO FOR YOUR GIRL SCOUT COUNCIL

Name: _____
_____

Can help with: _____
_____
_____
_____

Phone: _____

E-mail: _____
_____

SAY	INSTEAD OF
She has autism.	She's autistic.
She has an intellectual disability.	She's mentally retarded.
She has a learning disability.	The girl is learning-disabled.
She uses a wheelchair.	She is wheelchair-bound.
She has a disability.	She is handicapped.

Learn What a Girl Needs

Probably the most important thing you can do is to ask the individual girl or her parents or guardians what she needs to make her experience in Girl Scouts successful. If you are frank with the girl and her parents and make yourself accessible to them, it's likely they will respond in kind, creating a better experience for all.

It's important for all girls to be rewarded based on their best efforts—not on completion of a task. Give any girl the opportunity to do her best and she will. Sometimes that means changing a few rules or approaching an activity in a more creative way. Here are a few examples:

• Invite a girl to perform an activity after observing others doing it first.

• Ask the girls come up with ideas on how to adapt an activity.

Often what counts most is staying flexible and varying your approach. For a list of resources, visit www.girlscouts.org and search on "disability resources."

Snacking Smart Along the Quest

If the Brownies meet after school, they'll likely need a snack. Encourage members of your Brownie Family and Friends Network to take turns providing snacks, and remind them to think about snacking smart. Treats don't have to be frosted or fried to be special. Consider asking Network members to bring:

• Slices of fruit floating in a pitcher of water for refreshment along the Quest

• Carrots and other veggies dipped in natural, low-fat dressing

• Apple slices or banana chunks

• Low-fat cheese sticks and baked chips or crackers

• Cupfuls of trail mix with dried fruit and nuts

• Yogurt cups or mini fruit shakes

Check in with Brownie families about any food allergies or food issues.

Understanding the Journey's Leadership Benefits

Though filled with fun and friendship, the Brownie Quest is designed to develop the skills and values young girls need to be leaders in their own lives and as they grow. Girl Scouts of the USA has identified 15 national outcomes, or benefits, of the Girl Scout Leadership Experience. Activities on the Brownie Quest are designed to enable second- and third-grade girls to achieve nine of these outcomes, as detailed in the chart on the next page. You can notice the "signs" of these benefits throughout the journey.

Each girl is different, so don't expect them all to exhibit the same signs to indicate what they are learning along the journey. What matters is that you are guiding the Brownies toward leadership skills and qualities they can use right now—and all their lives.

For definitions of the outcomes and the signs that Girl Scout Brownies are achieving them, see the chart on the next page or *Transforming Leadership: Focusing on Outcomes of the New Girl Scout Leadership Experience* (GSUSA, 2008). Keep in mind that the intended benefits to girls are the cumulative result of traveling through an entire journey—and everything else girls experience in Girl Scouting.

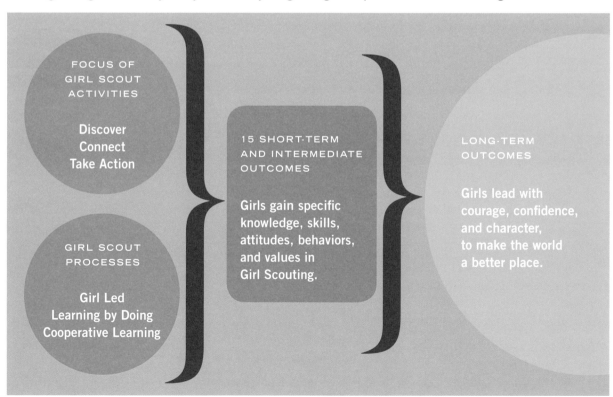

FOCUS OF GIRL SCOUT ACTIVITIES

**Discover
Connect
Take Action**

GIRL SCOUT PROCESSES

**Girl Led
Learning by Doing
Cooperative Learning**

15 SHORT-TERM AND INTERMEDIATE OUTCOMES

Girls gain specific knowledge, skills, attitudes, behaviors, and values in Girl Scouting.

LONG-TERM OUTCOMES

Girls lead with courage, confidence, and character, to make the world a better place.

NATIONAL LEADERSHIP OUTCOMES

	AT THE BROWNIE LEVEL, girls...	RELATED ACTIVITIES	SAMPLE "SIGN" When the outcome is achieved, girls might...
DISCOVER / **Girls develop a strong sense of self.**	have increased confidence in their abilities.	"Discovering Me" (Session 1). "Taking Action" (Sessions 5-6).	express pride in their accomplishments when speaking with others.
Girls develop positive values.	begin to apply values inherent in the Promise and Law in various contexts.	"Discovering Family" (Sessions 1-2: Sharing values of GS Law with family).	explain how they will take responsibility on the playground, at home, and at school.
Girls gain practical life skills— girls practice healthy living.	are better at making healthy choices and minimizing unhealthy behaviors.	"What's Happening at Campbell's House" and "Leading Your Family to Health" action (Sessions 2-3).	name healthy choices they make (e.g., walking every day, choosing healthful snacks).
Girls develop healthy relationships.	begin to understand how their behavior contributes to healthy relationships.	"Leading Your Family to Health" (Sessions 2-3).	identify healthy/unhealthy behaviors (e.g., honesty, caring, bullying) when presented with a relationship scenario.
CONNECT / **Girls promote cooperation and team-building.**	gain a better understanding of cooperative and team-building skills.	"Team Agreement" (Session 2) and follow-up reflections on keeping agreement. "Brownie Team Trade" (Session 4).	describe ways to make projects more fun (e.g., switching roles, brainstorming, listening to each other).
Girls feel connected to their communities locally and globally.	recognize the importance of being part of a larger community.	"Caring for Community" (Session 3). Take Action Project (Sessions 5-6).	give examples of how group/ community members help and support each other (e.g., in their neighborhood, school).
TAKE ACTION / **Girls can identify community needs.**	develop basic strategies to identify community issues.	Creating and doing the Take Action Project (Sessions 4-6).	list things about their community that are valuable and things that could be improved.
Girls educate and inspire others to act.	can communicate their reasons for engaging in community service and action.	Creating and doing the Take Action Project (Sessions 4-6).	explain why they chose a community action project (e.g., meals to seniors, holiday gifts to needy children), how/why it benefited others, and what they learned from it.
Girls feel empowered to make a difference.	increasingly feel they have important roles and responsibilities in their groups and/or communities.	"Caring for Community" (Session 3). Brownie Brainstorm (Session 4). Take Action Project (Sessions 5-6).	describe ways their actions contributed to bettering something (for their families, neighborhoods, environment).

Your Perspective on Leadership

The Girl Scout Leadership philosophy—Discover + Connect + Take Action—implies that leadership happens from the inside out. As the Quest ends, the Brownies will see that when they combine discovering, connecting, and taking action, they *are* leaders.

Your thoughts, enthusiasm, and approach will influence the Brownies all along the Quest, so take some time to reflect on your own perspective on leadership. Take a few minutes now—and throughout the Quest—to apply the "three keys of leadership" to yourself.

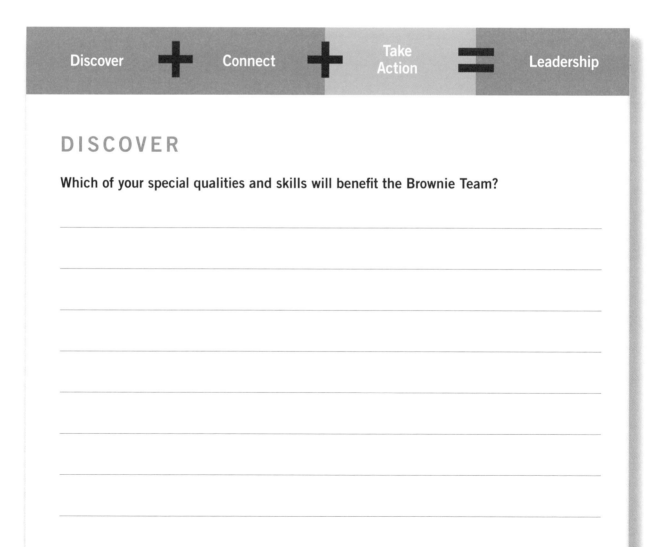

| Discover | **+** | Connect | **+** | Take Action | **=** | Leadership |

DISCOVER

Which of your special qualities and skills will benefit the Brownie Team?

What new qualities and skills are you discovering on this Quest?

_____

_____

_____

_____

_____

When you read the Girl Scout Law, what line most resonates with you? How does this strengthen your partnership with the Brownies?

_____

_____

_____

_____

CONNECT

Can you recall a great experience you had as part of a team?

_____

_____

_____

_____

_____

_____

_____

How did the team members connect to make it a great experience?

_____

_____

_____

_____

_____

_____

How does this memory inspire your efforts to guide the Brownies to connect as a Team?

_____

_____

_____

_____

_____

_____

TAKE ACTION

Why did you choose to volunteer with Girl Scouts?

_____

_____

_____

_____

_____

How does your volunteerism contribute to making the world a better place?

_____

_____

_____

_____

_____

How is Taking Action with the Brownies meaningful for you?

_____

_____

_____

_____

_____

"Brownies begin to see the world in which we live and it is not always a perfect picture. We get to help them navigate that world. We can start to give them the tools that they will need to meet life's challenges." —Angela Soden, Girl Scout volunteer and alumna, Blaine, Minnesota

THE JOURNEY'S SAMPLE SESSIONS

The sample sessions in this guide organize the Brownie Quest into seven meetings of about an hour each, with an option for containing the Quest within six sessions. As you travel along the Quest, be sure to read each session in full ahead of time. Envisioning each session in its entirety will help you make it come alive for the girls.

Keep in mind, too, that you can adjust the sessions—or the entire Quest—based on the girls' interest and availability. For those who have the time or desire to "linger," there are many ways to extend the Quest. The girls might:

- spend time together reading "The ELF Adventure," making up and even acting out alternate endings

- partner on Quest book games and activities

- spend more time on their Take Action Project

- organize an ending celebration with assistance from the Brownie Family and Friends Network (the girls might like to sing some Brownie songs or make a skit to go with the Brownie Ballad)

- create their own cheer to close out the Quest

- dream up other wonderful options

Tips for Working with the Sample Sessions

What You'll Find in Each Session

At a Glance: The session's goal and activities, a list of simple materials you'll need, and Advance Prep suggestions to help make the session a success.

What to Say: Examples of what to say and ask the Brownies along the Quest as you link activities, reflection, and learning experiences. Must you read from the "script"? Absolutely not! The girls (and you!) will have far more fun if you take the main ideas from the examples provided and then just be yourself.

Activity Instructions: Tips for guiding the girls through activities and experiences along the Quest, and plenty of "tools" (activity sheets, family notes, etc.) to correspond to the experiences on the Quest.

Coaching to Create a Quality Experience: The quality of the New Girl Scout Leadership Experience depends greatly on three processes—Girl Led, Cooperative Learning, and Learning by Doing. Just by following the prompts in this guide for activities, reflections, girl choice-making, and discussions, you'll be using the processes—with ease.

Send It Home: At the end of a few sessions, the Brownies plan a small activity to do at home with their families. All the activity sheets and instructions to send home are right here in your guide, along with handouts for your own use.

Tying Activities to Impact: This guide notes the purpose of the Quest's activities and discussions, so you'll always understand the intended benefit to the girls. You'll even be able to see the benefits—by observing the "signs" that the girls are achieving the Girl Scout National Leadership Outcomes.

Memory Keepers: Suggestions for simple mementos or souvenirs the girls can add to their Brownie Quest book to remember their experiences and new friends along the Quest.

Creative Detours

Think of these sample sessions as a road map to the Quest—they will get you and the girls from each step to the next, accomplishing goals along the way. As on any road trip, if you and your passengers have the time, use your imagination to "get off the highway" now and then to stop at your own roadside attractions. Consider, for example:

Trips

Since the Brownies are on a quest, play up the search factor by seeking assistance from the Brownie Family and Friends Network to visit zoos, botanical gardens, or other sites where the girls can get a map and then use it to explore and seek out information. Or consider having a fun day with a scavenger hunt at a Girl Scout camp property. You might also visit sites the Brownies have expressed interest in for their Take Action Project. Zoos and gardens will also give the girls a chance to map out important community places, and spark conversations about caring for animals or the environment. The fictional Brownie friends—Campbell, Jamila, and Alejandra—save a "tree family," so perhaps you might visit a place in your area where the real Brownies can embrace a tree family.

Making Things

Many Brownies love to create, so, depending on their interests, add a little time to a session (or add a whole session) to make a craft, recipe, or other project that girls can give as a gift or enjoy themselves. And don't feel you need to do it all yourself. Ask "craft-y" parents or other relatives to assist with projects related to the theme of the day's meeting. For example, perhaps some teens can assist the Brownies in making friendship bracelets. (The teens will be building leadership skills, too!)

Outdoor Time

Many of the suggested games and activities can be done outdoors. If the Brownie Team has access to outdoor space, play some games outside. The scavenger hunt in Session 1 is a great opportunity for the girls to be outside and on the move, and the closing ceremony could take place at a park. And keep in mind that Girl Scout councils often have wonderful camp properties that you may be able to use for a day.

WORKING WITHIN 7 SESSIONS

What if . . . there isn't enough time for even just the session activities . . . the girls don't seem to be enjoying something . . . some girls miss sessions . . . or families can't be involved beyond six sessions? Not to worry! By noting the intended purpose of the Quest's activities and discussions, you can make adjustments and still benefit the girls. As the Quest unfolds, you'll also have a sense of what the girls like, and you'll guide the sessions accordingly.

SAMPLE SESSION 1
Discovering . . . You, Values, Family

AT A GLANCE

Goal: Girl Scout Brownies discover and give voice to their special qualities and appreciate the qualities of their sister Brownies. Then they "find" the values of the Girl Scout Law and prepare to share them with their families.

- Ball Toss: Brownies introduce themselves and name their skills and qualities.

- Going ELF: Brownies search for values of the Girl Scout Law.

- Send It Home: Brownies discover their families' special qualities and the value of the Law that resonates most with them.

MATERIALS

- Girls' book and this guide

- Quest Master Map (display size)

- Optional: markers, glitter, glue, etc.

- Light ball (for Ball Toss)

- Poster board or large sheet of paper with star traced on it and names of the girls written in the star

- Clues (for the Search): Write each of the 10 values of the Girl Scout Law on paper and cut them into strips, or copy them from page 54 and cut them out. Number them 1 through 10 according to their place in the Girl Scout Law. Then paste

them on cards, or, if you have time, roll up each clue like a scroll and tie it with a ribbon, or put each card in a small cup or baggie.

- Optional: prizes/treats (stickers, pencils, key chains, healthy snacks)

- Copies of the Take-Home Letter and Making a Family Star activity sheet (pages 53-55, one set for each girl)*

*Note: The girls have a Family Star activity page in their books, but ideally they will carry home the photocopied page and create a free-standing star (maybe even a 3-D one!) with their families. But if it's easier, you could ask the families to use the star in the book.

ADVANCE PREP

- Chat with any assistants about who will do what before and during the session.

- Display your Quest Master Map in the meeting room to show the girls their progress when the session ends.

- Photocopy the activity sheets on pages 53-55.

AS GIRLS ARRIVE

Ask the girls to fill in some of the blanks in the "Discovering Me" activity on page 49 of their Brownie Quest book. This will get them thinking about their talents and personal qualities—useful info for their first Brownie Circle.

Now is also a great time for Cadette or adult helpers to circulate, introduce themselves, and assist the Brownies, as needed, in reading and filling in the blanks. Magic Markers, stickers, or other quick and easy decorations will add to the fun. The girls don't need to finish the activity page. Just thinking through a few responses will enable them to call out their talents and qualities during the Ball Toss.

Setting Up the Search

A special part of Session 1 is the "search" for the values of the Girl Scout Law. You can make this part of the Quest as elaborate as time and resources allow. What matters is providing the girls with a physical opportunity to search. Here are some tips to bring the search to life:

TAKE IT OUTSIDE

If time, weather, and support from other adults permit, plan for an outdoor search. By following *Safety-Wise* and any other information your Girl Scout council has about trips and the outdoors, you'll ensure that the girls stay safe while having a great time.

USE YOUR MEETING SPACE CREATIVELY

If you decide to stick to your usual meeting place, think about how and where you can create a short and fun search for the girls. You or a helper could arrive a few minutes early to hide the clues. Or perhaps a helper can occupy the girls with music or singing while you hide them.

YOUR GROUP'S SIZE

The Brownies will "link arms" to search for clues, so keep in mind the Team's size. Every pair or threesome will want to discover at least one clue. So unless the group is quite small, instruct each pair or trio to sit down as soon as they've found two clues. For large groups, consider blocking off areas of your meeting space so multiple searches can run at the same time—or just hide multiple sets of clues.

EXTRAS

"Rev up" the fun factor by adding small prizes or treats (stickers, pencils, key chains, healthy snacks) to the clues. Just be sure to keep a few minutes at the end of the session for the Brownies to talk about finding the values of the Girl Scout Law.

Ball Toss: Discovering Our Special Talents and Qualities

In this game, the girls discover and name some of their special talents or qualities, and then discover and appreciate what other girls bring to the Brownie Circle. Plus, they can release a little energy!

Begin by gathering the girls into a circle and welcoming them to the Girl Scout Brownie Quest.

Say something like:

- *When we join in a Girl Scout Brownie Circle, we're making connections with millions of girls all over the world standing in Brownie Circles just like this one. Imagine 500,000 girls doing this same thing—you are part of this amazing sisterhood!*

- *Every time we create our Brownie Circle, we can imagine that it is like a giant tree house—where Girl Scout Brownies around the world belong together.*

- *Today, we are using our Brownie Circle as the start to our special Quest to find three keys. There are three steps we have to take to find each key. Ready for the first step toward the first key?*

- *The first step is to discover all the skills and talents and qualities each of us brings with us on our Quest. So, as we toss the ball around our circle, say your name and one special skill or talent or quality that you can bring into our Brownie Circle.*

- *I'll start: My name is _____ and I have a lot of energy, so I never give up!*

As the girls toss the ball around, encourage them to describe their qualities and talents. If they get stuck, read out lines from the "Discovering Me" activity page and have the girls fill in the blanks.

Record (or ask a Brownie friend or family member to record) what the girls say. Do this inside the large star you sketched on poster board or newsprint. Label it "Discovering Ourselves." At upcoming sessions, this will be a good visual reminder of what the girls discovered about themselves at the Quest's start. *Option:* Invite the girls to decorate the Brownie Team star as the meeting ends or at the beginning of the next session. Then display it each time the Team meets and at a closing celebration.

When everyone has had a few turns tossing and catching, wind down by summarizing the qualities and talents the girls bring to their Brownie Circle.

BE YOURSELF

As always, feel free to use your own words to make these points that open the Quest!

Consider ending the activity with a friendship squeeze. Ask the girls to silently appreciate the qualities of the girl next to them as they pass along the squeeze.

Going ELF: The Search to Discover the Values of the Girl Scout Law

In this activity, the girls deepen their awareness of the Girl Scout Law by searching for, discovering, and then talking about the Law's values. With the search, the girls also begin the tradition of "ELF" (Explore, Link Arms, and Fly into Action).

Introduce the search by saying something like:

- *One step we already took to find the first key today was discovering our special talents and qualities. How many more steps do we have to take to find the first key? (Two!) (Mark it on the Quest Master Map.)*

- *Now it's time for the second step! There are some important clues to the first key hidden all around this area. (Add a descriptor such as, "They are all tied with a red ribbon.") You need to find the clues and put them together to discover what they mean.*

- *But before you start searching, you need to know about an important tradition for Girl Scout Brownies—and that's "ELF." What does that stand for?*

- *We have a secret meaning for "ELF" here in the Brownie Tree House. Only girls on this Quest know the real meaning:*

> **E**xplore
> **L**ink Arms
> **F**ly into Action

- *So you need to "go ELF!" to find those clues. You are going to go Exploring by Linking Arms* (at the elbow) *with a partner* (or in threes). *Then, listen for my special "Fly into Action" instructions as you look for the clues.* (Give any other instructions needed, such the number of clues you want each pair/threesome to find, what the girls should do once they find the clues—sit and read them, etc.).

Then tell the girls, *OK, ready, set, start the Quest.*

As the girls move about, give special "Fly into Action" instructions like:

• *Skip around with your arms linked while you search.*

• *Now hop around and keep hopping even if you are picking up a clue.*

• *Remember to stay linked.*

• *Flap your free arms—pretend you are flying!*

When all the "clues" have been found, ask the girls to "unlink" and return to their Brownie Circle. Ask partners and threesomes to share clues so every girl has one clue in hand. Or, in large groups, perhaps every team can share a clue. In small teams, Brownie helpers can step in to hold clues. Keep the end of the search moving at a good clip so you keep the energy and attention of the Brownie Team!

Say:

• *Now I'm going to call on you based on the clue number you found.*

• *Will number 1 come forward?*

• *Will number 2 come forward and link arms with number 1?*

• *Will number 3 come forward and link up?*

. . . and so on, until all numbers, 1 through 10, are accounted for and the girls are linked into one big chain. In large groups, you might have multiple girls holding each numbered clue. In that case, have all the number 1s start a chain and then have all the number 2s link with them, and so on, until the girls end up in one big chain.

Then say:

All the number 1s, please read your clue aloud.

Number 2s?

Work your way up to number 10, so that the entire Girl Scout Law is read aloud.

Then say:

What do all these clues add up to? "The Girl Scout Law!" (The girls may answer or you may need to tell them.)

Explain why the Girl Scout Law matters.

You might say:

Each line of the Girl Scout Law represents a value—something we believe is important and that we try to live by. Our values are part of what make us special—just like all the talents and qualities you shared in the Brownie Circle today.

Next, give the girls time to do the "Discovering Values" activity on page 50 of their Quest book.

Winding Down from the Search

If you have time, end by reading Chapter 1 of the story, starting on page 10 of the girls' book. Or ask the girls to volunteer to read parts of the story. Or simply encourage the girls to read the story at home with a family member.

Wind up the session by saying something like:

We're getting ready to leave the Brownie Tree House for today. We'll open it up again for the next session. But before we go, let's take a minute and think about how far we've already traveled on the Brownie Quest!

If you have your Quest Master Map on display, fill in the spaces as you ask the girls to recap and prepare for a family activity.

Say something like:

We took the first two steps to finding the first key!

What was the first step? (Discovering our talents and qualities.)

What was the second step? (Discovering the values of the Girl Scout Law.)

Now you can choose to accept the Quest. And then there's just one step to go—and you get to do that at home with your families!

You will take a star and fly into action by discovering some of the special talents and qualities in your family. Don't forget to ask your family what value of the Girl Scout Law is most important for them!

Send It Home

Hand out the stars and the "Making a Family Star" page and letter. Remind the girls to bring the Family Star to the next session. Say good-bye and then pat yourself on the back! Congratulations! You've got the Brownies going ELF!

MEMENTOS OF THE QUEST

Creating visual and written mementos is a vital part of the Brownie Quest. Mementos remind the girls of their explorations—and they'll love putting keepsakes in the Making Memories section of their Quest books.

For the girls' first memento, ahead of Session 2 create (or ask a helper to create) a list of the girls' first names; next to each name list some of the qualities and talents discovered in Session 1.

Make copies and present this "Discovering Us" list to the girls during Session 2, offering them an opportunity to decorate this memento and place it in their Brownie Quest books, perhaps upon arrival or as the session ends.

Discovering Family: Take-Home Letter and Activity

The following pages hold the Brownie Family Star Take-Home Letter and the Discovering Family activity, including a star for the girls and their families to fill in. You can photocopy these pages and give one set to each girl to take home with her at the end of the session.

Girl Scout Brownie Quest

Assist Your Brownie in Her Quest!

Dear Girl Scout Brownie Family:

During your Girl Scout Brownie's first adventure on the Brownie Quest, she discovered some of the talents and qualities that make her special. Check out page 49 of her Brownie Quest book to see how she describes herself!

At her next Girl Scout session, your Brownie will earn the Brownie Quest's very first key. But first she has one important step to take—and she needs your help.

Read the questions on the accompanying activity sheet and assist your Brownie in writing, and talking about, some simple answers to put on her star. This is a great time for you to talk with your Brownie about a value of the Girl Scout Law that is important in your family. Try to give your Brownie an example of what it means to act on a value described in the Law (such as being honest or courageous).

Your Brownie has a family star on page 51 of her Quest book—that's for her to keep. The enclosed activity sheet is for you to use with your Brownie. Or feel free to create a unique star of your own with your Brownie, using a paper plate, cardboard, aluminum foil—whatever's handy. Your Brownie will have more fun if you make a 3-D star! But if you don't have a lot of time, just use the one provided or stick with the star in your Brownie's Quest book.

If you have time, ask your Brownie to read "The ELF Adventure" with you—even just the first chapter. (See pages 10-15 in your Brownie's Quest book.) Talk about what parts interest your Brownie.

Thank you!

Making a Family Star

Read the Girl Scout Law with your family:

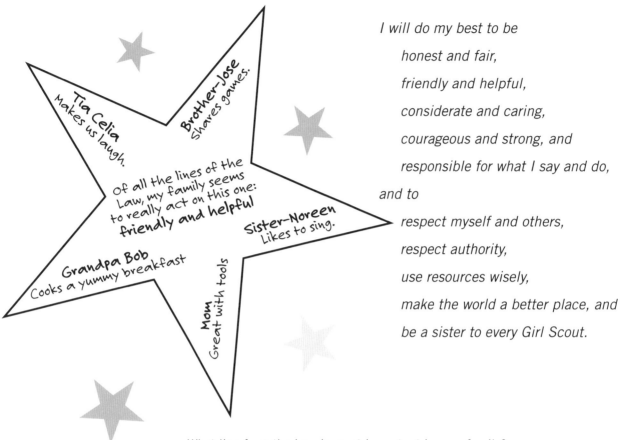

Tia Celia
Makes us laugh.

Brother-Jose
Shares games.

Of all the lines of the Law, my family seems to really act on this one:
friendly and helpful

Sister-Noreen
Likes to sing.

Grandpa Bob
Cooks a yummy breakfast

Mom
Great with tools

I will do my best to be

honest and fair,

friendly and helpful,

considerate and caring,

courageous and strong, and

responsible for what I say and do,

and to

respect myself and others,

respect authority,

use resources wisely,

make the world a better place, and

be a sister to every Girl Scout.

What line from the Law is most important in your family?

Why?

Write your family's favorite line and the reason why in the center of your star.

Here's an example:

Courageous

Sometimes it is hard to do what you know is right—that's why being courageous is so important!

Who is in your family (mother, father, grandfather, aunt, sisters, brothers)? Write their names in the points of your star.

What special quality or skill do your family members have? Write those under their names.

After you fill in your star, decorate it if you want to! Add colors, stickers, glitter, or whatever else you have handy and bring it to your next Brownie session!

My Family Star

"Don't be afraid to mix old treasures
with new adventures."

—Grandmother Elf in "The ELF Adventure"

SAMPLE SESSION 2
Discovering and Connecting

AT A GLANCE

Goal: The girls engage in a team-building game and reflect on the experience, which guides them to create a Brownie Team Agreement—the first step to the second key.

- Brownie Star Circle: Brownies share their family discoveries and join in the first Quest ceremony, earning the Discover Key.

- Connecting as a Team: Brownies play a cooperative game and then create their own Team Agreement.

- Send It Home: The girls follow Brownie Friend Campbell's example and commit to leading a healthy-living activity with their families.

MATERIALS

- Brownie Team "Discovering Us" list (if you chose to make copies of the list of the girls' talents in Session 1)

- "Discovering Ourselves" board (if made in Session 1)

- Quest Master Map (for display)

- Glue stick or tape, stickers, markers or crayons

- Extra photocopies of the star in case a girl forgets hers

- Discover Keys (if planning to give out this award) or paper keys or stickers to represent the award milestone and, if desired, photocopies of the Discover Chant (page 91)

- Copies (and examples) of "Connect at Home" projects for the girls to do with families

- A hula hoop or ball, depending on what team game you choose

- Large sheet of paper for the Team Agreement. Or trace a large circle (the icon for "Connect") on the board.

- Copies of letter for the Brownies to take home

Brownie Star Circle and Discover Key Ceremony

Ask the Brownies to form a circle, with each girl placing her star on the floor in front of her. Invite each girl to say something about her family star; encourage a discussion of values, and link the conversation to the Girl Scout Law by saying something like:

- *We each created stars that show the people in our families and the special talents they have.*

- *We also talked to our families about the values we learned in the Girl Scout Law and which values are important to our families.*

- *What line or value of the Girl Scout Law did you talk about with your family?*

- *Would someone else like to share the value your family talked about and put in your star?*

After all the girls have had a chance to speak, invite them to appreciate all the talents and values they have brought into the Brownie Circle with their family stars.

Try:

- Walking around the Brownie Circle together, pausing to read (or inviting the girls to read) each star.

- Inviting the girls to pass their stars around the circle, allowing a minute or two between each "pass" for the girls to look at each other's stars.

STAR POWER

If your Brownie Team is large, you could have a few circles going—and an assistant or two. This will ensure that each girl gets ample time to share her thoughts about her Family Star.

Yoo-hoo, Brownie Elf, where's our family star?

Wrap up the discussion by inviting the girls into a short ceremony to celebrate finding the first key. Use the Quest Master Map to show the girls their progress as you reflect with them about the steps they took to find the key.

Say:

So far we have:

1. Discovered our special talents and qualities.

2. Discovered the values of the Girl Scout Law.

3. And just now, we discovered our family talents and values.

We completed three steps! That means we have found the first key. What do you think the first key is called?

The first key is the Discover Key! And we are going to have a special celebration because you found it!

STAR CELEBRATION

In their Quest books, the girls have a page to note what they put in their family star. So they may let you keep their Brownie Stars for the closing celebration, where their families and friends can appreciate them.

Ceremony

In the circle, join hands around the Brownie Star Circle.

Say something like:

Each Girl Scout Brownie here has earned the Discover Key because you … discovered yourself and your values—as a Girl Scout and a member of your family. Say or chant after me (have the girls repeat each line as a team after you or your helpers say it once):

*The Discover Key
It's all about me:
What I believe
And my family.*

Perhaps invite the girls to repeat the chant a few times—getting louder each time—and end with a round of applause.

Distribute the Discover Keys, inviting the girls to add them to their vests or sashes as an official Girl Scout Brownie award!

Pass out copies of the Discover Chant (you can photocopy it from page 91). The girls can decorate it and place it in their book now or later at home. Or invite the girls to write the chant in their book, on page 52.

Connecting as a Team

Keep the energy going by saying something like:

- *Now that you have found the Discover Key, you can move ahead and find the second key. Is everyone ready? How many steps are there to find each key? (Three.)*

- *The first step to finding that second key is to practice our Brownie Team skills. When we join together, we make a very strong Girl Scout Brownie ELF Team. This game is going to help us think about how we need to act together to be a great team.*

Give the instructions for the "team-building" game (see the bottom of this page and the next for the games).

Play the game! Then invite the girls back to the Brownie Circle. Coach them to reflect on how they acted like a Team during the game.

Try questions and prompts such as:

- *What are some of the things you did to help each other (pass the ball or hoop)?*

  Look at each other

  Help each other

  Listen

- *Did you need to trust each other? Why? Was that hard or easy?*

- *What happens on a team if someone makes a mistake? Do we want that person to feel bad? What can we do?*

- *What makes being on a team together fun?*

- *What would make us feel bad about being on the Brownie Team together?*

LOOP THE HOOP*

Four or more players try to move the hoop from player to player without letting go of each others' hands.

Materials: One or more hula hoops (depending on size of group)

To play:

1. Players stand in a circle, holding hands.

2. Hang a hula hoop over one player.

3. While holding hands, players pass the hula hoop completely around the circle without letting it touch the ground.

Variation: For a large group, use two hoops, starting side by side, but going in different directions. The game ends when the two hula hoops meet.

Creating the Brownie Team Agreement

Say something like:

- *Strong teams have Team Agreements—or promises—about how team members cooperate together. We can use the examples we just talked about to write a Brownie Team Agreement for our time together in the Brownie Tree House and on our Quest.*

Write (or ask a helper to write) on poster board or cardboard the key words from the discussion—words important to girls when they think about being a strong team. Draw a circle around the words and label it "Brownie Team Agreement."

If the girls need prompting, suggest some agreement like:

On this Team, we think it is important to

> *Listen*

> *Help each other*

> *Let go of mistakes*

> *Talk kindly to one another*

> *Look at the person who is talking*

Some Brownies may want to volunteer to decorate the Team Agreement at the end of this session or the beginning of the next one. Bring it to upcoming sessions and use it to encourage the Brownies to reflect on their efforts at teamwork. (Perhaps also bring the Brownie Team Agreement to the closing celebration and have the Brownies discuss how they have tried to stick to it!)

The Brownies also have a Team Agreement form on page 53 of their Quest book. If girls want to, they can fill it out to reflect what they just decided as a team.

PASS THE BALL, PLEASE*

Five or more players try to pass a ball from one end of a line to the other end without using their hands or letting the ball touch the ground.

Materials: A ball (the smaller the ball, the more difficult)

To play:

1. Players sit on the floor in a line with their legs straight out.

2. The ball is placed between the ankles of the first girl, who, without touching it, passes it to the next girl.

3. If the ball touches the ground, the Team must begin again.

*From: *Let's Play Games for Girls Ages 5-11*, pages 34-35

Prepare to Connect at Home

This activity prepares girls to "care" for their families by leading a healthy-living project at home.

Transition by saying something like:

- *We've taken our first step to find the second key by _____ (creating a Brownie Team Agreement). Fill this in on the Quest Master Map you have displayed.*

- *Our Team Agreement shows how you care about and connect with each other. Who else do you care about? (The girls may call out members of their families and friends.)*

- *Showing our families we care about them is really important! So you are going to take the second step to finding the second key at home—with your families.*

Look at the picture "What's Happening at Campbell's House," on page 54 of the girls' book.

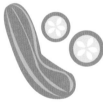

Ask the girls:

- *What could Campbell's family do to be really happy in their home?*

- *What might make them feel really good?*

- *What are some things in their house that might be stopping them from feeling good?*

Use the rest of the "What's Happening at Campbell's House?" activity on page 55 of the girls' book to engage the Brownies in more thinking about what it looks like to take great care of ourselves and our families.

Send It Home!

Ask the girls to look at the healthy-living suggestions on page 55 of their book. Then, say something like:

- *What would you like to take the lead on to show your family you care about them?*

- *Can we each make a promise to show our families we care by doing one thing from the healthy-living list at home?*

- *Write down what you do and bring it back the next time we meet.*

Girl Scout Brownie Quest

Healthy-Living Family Activity

Dear Girl Scout Brownie Family:

Your Brownie is practicing her leadership skills. An important one is showing that she cares about her family! Sometime before the next session, she will be leading you in a healthy-living activity.

A few healthy-living activities are listed below, but feel free to let the conversation with your Brownie guide you to a new activity! What matters is giving your Brownie a chance to take the lead and show how much she cares about her family. Once she has, help her fill out the Commitment Card at the end of this letter.

Possible Healthy-Living Actions

Find the healthy ideas and recipes in the Brownie Quest book. With your Brownie, pick one for your family.

Try a new healthy drink (for example, water or low-fat milk)

Be active together—walk, bike ride, or play catch or tag or another active game.

If your family already does many of these things, see how creative you can be with coming up with something new.

We look forward to hearing how your Brownie led your family!

Thank you!

Please have your Brownie return this Commitment Card to her next Girl Scout meeting.

COMMITMENT CARD

Brownie's Name

_____

_____

I showed my family I care about their health!

I led my family to be healthier by

_____

_____

_____

_____

_____

Brownie Signature

_____

Date

SAMPLE SESSION 3
Connecting and Taking Action

AT A GLANCE

Goal: Brownies earn the Connect Key by first exploring the "circles" of their lives and then expanding their caring to their community by writing a letter to a school or town official to seek a healthy-living improvement.

- Circle Map: Brownies explore how the "circles" of their lives grow outward: Me, Family, Girl Scouts, Community, World.

- Posting Commitments: In the map's Family circle, Brownies post Commitment Cards noting their family's healthy-living actions.

- Caring for Community: The Team expands its circle of caring through two stories—one real, one fictional— that serve as springboards to writing a letter to a school or town official to seek a healthy-living improvement.

- Earning the Connect Key: Brownies close with the Quest's second ceremony, earning their second key.

MATERIALS

- Quest Master Map (for display with "Discover" steps and first "Connect" step filled in)

- Copies of the Brownie Team Agreement

- Have blank copies of the Healthy Living Commitment Card (for those who've forgotten them)

- Tape

- Paper and envelopes (or, if you have a computer where you meet, use e-mail!)

- Connect Keys ready to distribute

- Copies of the chant (for the girls to add to their books)

Advance Prep

- Have copies of the Brownie Team Agreement ready so the girls can decorate, autograph, and add it to their Quest book as they arrive. (Option: Snap a photo of the Agreement and make copies.)

- Draw five concentric circles (they don't need to be perfect!) on a large sheet of paper (newsprint, poster board, butcher paper) or blackboard/whiteboard. Write "Me" in the center circle. (You'll add the other labels during the activity.)

- The girls will need to have their Healthy Living Commitment Cards, filled in with what they did to care for their families.

- For the letter-writing, bring (or ask a helper to get) contact information for local schools, the town mayor or another official, your Girl Scout council, or other organizations the girls might write to.

TIP

For groups larger than about 10 girls, have two or more circle map discussions going on at the same time on opposite sides of the room.

As the Girls Arrive

Memory Keepers: Provide copies of the Brownie Team Agreement and invite the girls to decorate, autograph, and insert it in their Quest book. They might also want to decorate the large version of the Agreement (from Session 2).

Check that the girls have their Healthy Living Commitment Cards or activity pages with them for the Caring for Community activity. Assist those who may have forgotten to fill one in.

Circle Map: Creating Circles of Caring

Gather the girls around the five concentric circles. Open with a quick refresher about where they are on the Quest by using your Master Map. Then take a few minutes to ask the girls about what other maps they've seen or know about.

Ask questions like:

> What key did we find already?
>
> What key are we looking for now? (The second!)
>
> How many steps do we have left before we find it? (Two!)
>
> Can anyone guess what the second key might be called? (No need to give the answer; just say: Interesting—we'll find out soon enough!)

Next, say something like:

> OK, here we go—our Quest begins again. We're going to make a new kind of map, using these circles. It will be a map about all the people we care about.

Point to the center circle and ask:

Why is "Me" in the center? What did we do that represents each of you? (Created Discover stars, representing our talents and values).

Point to the next circle and ask:

Which people are most important to you? (Write in "Family.")

Since our families are so important to us, we used our care skills to lead our families to better health. Each of you is going to place your Healthy Living card up here in that circle. And while you do, tell us what you did and how it went.

Once all the girls have added their cards to the Family Circle, say something like:

Congratulations! You each used your leadership skills to connect with your families in an important way! And that's the second step to the second key!

Point to the next circle and ask:

When we get together here, we belong to what? (The Girl Scout Brownie Circle or Sisterhood! That includes our circle here and the big circle of Girl Scouts all around the world.)

What did we do already to practice connecting as a Brownie Team? We made our Team Agreement (that was the first step of this second key we are looking for).

Point to the fourth circle and ask:

So who else do you care about? Guide the girls as they brainstorm—and write these "people in our community" in the fourth circle:

Friends and teachers at school

Relatives (beyond immediate family)

Neighbors

People at a place of worship/in a spiritual community

People at local businesses and stores

Perhaps the mail carrier or firefighters or police and others who take care of the community

Point to the fifth circle and ask:

And outside our communities, what do we have? The whole wide world!

Caring for Community

Since we've already done something for the "Me" circle and used our leadership with our families, and made our Brownie Team agreement, we are reaching out to that fourth circle—community.

Let's look at this true story about what one group of kids did to be leaders in their community.

Have the girls turn to "The Case of the Broken Sidewalk" on page 64 of their book. Invite them to take turns reading parts of the story aloud.

Guide the girls to reflect on how the kids in the story cared about a wider circle of people than just themselves.

Ask questions like:

- *Who did these kids worry about? When something happens to you or a friend or your family, do you worry that it could happen to someone else?*

- *Why did the kids decide to write a letter?*

- *What is the result of their writing the letter?*

Next ask the girls to think about the kinds of "healthy living" things they did with their families. Give examples of how some of these ideas could also benefit the wider community.

After the girls have had time to do some thinking about the problems in Green Falls, ask them to think about their own neighborhoods. Ask if there's anything that seems to need fixing there.

Examples:

- Maybe people need a space to take walks where cars are not going by.

- Maybe the community needs a bike path.

- Maybe the school needs an improved play area.

- Maybe the school needs to provide more water fountains or better snacks.

(See page 70 for a letter template the Brownies can adapt for their particular project. If you make copies for the girls, they can take it home and talk about their ideas with their families.)

Invite the girls (in small teams or one large group) to choose one idea and to think about who to write to about it—the school, the town, etc. Then have them

HAVE A LARGE GROUP?

Divide the girls into small teams and have a helper partner with each team to read and discuss the story and create a letter.

think about what they will write. Their letter can be simple and direct—just clear reporting on an important issue and expressing their desire to be part of the solution.

Brainstorm a few sentences and write the letter together. Have all the girls sign it. Say that you will send it.

Remind the girls that it takes time for big changes like this:

You might not see results right away, but by calling attention to it and trying to help, you are demonstrating leadership!

Say:

And that was the third step to the second key—connecting with others in telling and showing our community that we care!

Keep in mind that if the girls receive an answer, they might like to display the reply during their big Quest celebration that takes place in Session 7 (or at the end of Session 6).

Closing: Earning the Connect Key

Form a Brownie Circle and invite the girls to chant after you:

The Connect Key! That's more than me. It's my arms and your arms. Linking together, we're free.

Say:

Congratulations! You have earned the Connect Key. (Give out the key and a copy of the chant.)

Sample Letter to

Address a Community Project

(Name and Address of community official)

Dear [Ms. Mayor or . . .],

Who we are and where we're from
We live near (the place you will be talking about—for example, the Dolphin Park, at 13th Street and Summit Avenue). We have noticed this problem every day when we play at the park.

The problem
The park is very close to the street, and there is no safety fence around it. The kids' balls roll in the street all the time. When cars stop at the traffic light, some passengers shout at us when we're playing. The park doesn't feel safe. We think a fence around the park would make us feel safer.

Suggestion for a solution
The Girl Scouts in our group (name) have had many meetings about this park and feeling safe. We have learned that the office of the (official) can write the order for making the neighborhood and our park safe.

Time frame
That's why we are starting by asking you for help. We hope you can do it this year before spring comes and everyone's playing at the park again.

What we can do
This is what we can do to help:

- Make posters.
- Show neighbors that everyone needs to care about our park and about kids being safe.
- Ask neighbors to help plant bushes and flowers around the fence.
- Let neighbors know that you and your office helped to make our park safer.

Thank you for reading about the problem in our neighborhood. We hope you will help us and write back.

Sincerely,

(name of group)
(everyone signs letter)

"FLYING INTO ACTION" CHECKLIST

As the Girl Scout Brownie Team flies into action, use this checklist to maximize the impact on the girls and their community.

- [ ] The girls identify a variety of places or situations where they could be useful and think about who might need them and what they could do. (Session 4: Brownie Brainstorm, page 76.)

- [ ] The girls make a Team decision with backup plans! (Session 4: Brownie Team Trade, page 78.) *This is the first step toward the Take Action Key: The Brownies identify a problem they care about.*

- [ ] The girls prepare for the action while learning more about the problem they are addressing and how their efforts will make a difference. During this step, the girls meet people associated with the place they have chosen for their action. Interacting with others will deepen the Brownies' awareness of their communities. *This is the second step toward the Take Action Key: The Brownies plan and prepare.*

  An example of this step: The Brownies have chosen to take action with a food pantry. You arrange for them to meet with a volunteer from the pantry to learn more about hunger in the area and the kinds of food people need. The girls go on to make a list of the foods needed and create posters for a food drive.

- [ ] The girls Take Action. *This is the third step to earning the Take Action Key: improving the world!*

- [ ] The girls reflect on their project and add a memory keeper about it to their Quest books.

- [ ] The girls celebrate and earn the Take Action Key.

The girls **discover** how to use their skills and values in the world around them, **connect** with each other, and **take action** to improve the world. The girls are engaged as leaders! They're making it happen!

Preparing for Sample Session 4

Tips for Organizing the Take Action Project

During Session 4, you'll guide the Brownie Team to identify a place in the community where they want to Fly into Action and make a group decision about what they will do.

Then you will organize Sessions 5 and 6 based on the nature of the girls' project, practicalities (like the best day and time to carry out the project), and the time and resources your team of girls and supporters have available.

During these last three sessions, keep in mind your purpose: engaging the girls to the greatest extent possible in making their mark on the world. Seek every opportunity to relate what may seem like simple actions to the bigger intent.

GIRL LEADERSHIP AND GIRL CHOICE

The girls are getting ready to do a Take Action Project. Whether it's big or small, they will be identifying a problem they care about, brainstorming ideas for solving it, and making decisions along the way—all important leadership skills for the girls to practice along this Brownie Quest. The goal is to coach the girls on a thought process that will stick with them for years to come—and potentially have far greater impact than the one community project they tackle now.

So resist any temptation to find a place in your community that needs some help and set everything up for the Brownies. Remember: It's their Take Action Project!

Keeping in mind the various kinds of action that are possible will be useful as you guide the girls in their project brainstorm. They may, for example, suggest an action that might not be feasible, but you may be able to prompt them to think about an alternate but related action that addresses the same issue from another angle.

Keep the checklist on the previous page and examples of various types of projects handy as you proceed along the final sessions of the Quest.

How the Brownies Might Take Action

There are many ways to take action to improve the world. Make this a meaningful effort for the Brownies by engaging them in a project that goes beyond collecting supplies or cleaning up. Use your Flying into Action Checklist to ensure that the girls choose a quality and age-appropriate project.

Here are some examples of what the Brownies' action might be:

- **Possible action:** The Brownies make several storybooks (or one big one) to give and read to nursery school children at a local day-care center or shelter. They also practice a song or game to teach younger kids or pack healthy snacks to share. And they talk to the staff or volunteers to understand why their visit is special for the children.

- **Possible action:** The Brownies meet a nutrition specialist to talk about what food groups make up a healthy meal and then gather donations for a local food pantry. (Have you ever tried to make a meal from canned tuna, canned beans, cereal, and peanut butter? Those are examples of the donations that often arrive at a food pantry. So perhaps the Brownies can organize a more complete and healthier selection of donations!)

- **Possible action:** The Brownies learn about healthy eating tips for themselves and then create a presentation for their schools or for a gathering of families and friends. Or the girls interview local experts and then create a presentation about saving water and energy that they will share with their schools, church groups, or other Girl Scout groups.

- **Possible action:** The Brownies write letters and talk to someone about a bigger problem they want their town or school or some other group to pay attention to. This is what the kids in Ms. Jeanne's class did—and perhaps the Brownies would like to use this example and do something beyond Session 3's basic letter-writing, such as arranging a visit with someone who could influence the challenge they want to address.

Perhaps the girls are doing something unique that you and they brainstormed about together to make the world a better place.

FOLLOWING THE BROWNIE FRIENDS

In "The ELF Adventure" story, Campbell, Jamila, and Alejandra pursue a "Save the Trees" action that improves the environment. They also educate and inspire others in the community and advocate for a new approach. As you learn about what interests your Brownie Team, consider how blending various types of possible actions together will enrich their experience!

What could it mean — this E-L-F?
Were there elves somewhere to find?
Yes! That's it! That's the key!
It's a message meant to mind!

—From the Brownie Ballad

SAMPLE SESSION 4
Choosing a Take Action Project

AT A GLANCE

Goal: Brownie Team members identify a community need that matters to them and begin to create a solution—a way to Fly into Action and accomplish something on behalf of others.

- Brownie Brainstorm: Team members consider community places where they could Take Action to make a difference.

- Brownie Team Trade: The Team "goes ELF" while deciding on top ideas for taking action.

- Brownie Plan: The Team talks about preparations and materials they need to Take Action.

MATERIALS

- Brownie Brainstorm Chart, a big chart for posting the girls' brainstorming ideas (see sample chart, page 77)

- Whiteboard/chalkboard and chalk, butcher paper you can tape on a wall, or poster board

- Markers

- Sticky notes or small slips of paper for writing Team Trades

ADVANCE PREP

The Brownie Brainstorm Chart **Create the framework for a Brownie Brainstorm Chart (see the sample chart on page 77), including column headings, ahead of time. The starting point for the brainstorming is the "Place" column (cover the last two columns until you get to the Brainstorm), so don't fill in the places. That's the first question you'll ask the girls. Make the chart as big as possible so the Brownies can put their "trades" on it.**

As Girls Arrive

Invite the Brownies to add a copy of the Team letter created in Session 3 to the Making Memories pages of their Quest book. Also invite the girls to read "The ELF Adventure" and think (and talk) about how Campbell, Jamila, and Alejandra are taking action in Green Falls.

Brownie Brainstorm: Who Needs the Brownie ELF Team and What Can We Do for Them?

Welcome the girls back to the Quest! Invite them to share a favorite part of the Quest so far and to consider their Brownie Team Agreement before they begin today.

Show the girls the Quest Master Map—and their progress: They've found both the Discover Key and the Connect Key, and they're starting on the third key! What do they think the name of the third key is?

Then say something like:

> *Here we go! Our first step toward the third key is figuring out who needs some help from our Brownie Team. Where can we Fly into Action and make the world a better place?*
>
> *Let's think about all the places in our neighborhood where people might need us to do something for them. How many places can we think of where people might need the Brownies to Fly into Action?*

Brownie Brainstorm

Using the big version of the Brownie Brainstorm Chart that you created, guide the girls to brainstorm places where people need some Brownie ELF action.

- Give hints for the many places the girls could be needed.

- Fill in the "places" in the first column of your Brownie Brainstorm Chart. (You needn't include everything mentioned on the sample chart.)

- Move to the next column and keep the Brownie Brainstorm going! Coach the girls to think about both the people who work at the places that might need their action and the people who are served by those places.

- Move to the third column. What actions could the girls take? (Stretch the girls' thinking by giving hints related to "educating and inspiring" and "advocating.")

Now it's time to transition to girl decision-making!

REMEMBER THE TAKE ACTION EXAMPLES . . .

. . . like the one in "The Case of the Broken Sidewalk." The girls might write a letter, give a presentation, or talk to someone in charge. Feel free to capture more than one "what could the Brownie Team do" idea in each part of the chart because some ideas might not prove feasible.

Brownie Brainstorm Chart

Place*	Who might need you?	What could the Brownie ELF Team do?	What do you need to find out?	What supplies would you need?
Nursery School or Day-Care Program	Little kids who want to play and meet a new friend.			
Library				
Hospital				
Food Pantry				
Fire Station				
Emergency Housing Shelter				
Playground or Park				
Girl Scout Program Centers				
Veterans Hospital or Center				

*The places in this column are just examples. Fill in this column with ideas from the girls. If needed, give them some hints to get them started.

Brownie Team Trade: Brownies Link Arms to Make a Team Decision

The purpose of this activity is to coach the Brownies to decide on a Flying into Action project that they all are excited about. If you are pressed for time, a simple "show of hands" vote, with some discussion and compromise conversation, will get you there. You'll deepen the experience by giving the girls an opportunity to care about and support the ideas of their teammates. So try an approach like this (it gets everyone moving around, too!):

Divide the Brownie Team into pairs, encouraging the girls to partner with someone "new." Ask the pairs to link arms. Have all the pairs stand together in a circle, and give each pair two sticky notes (or two pieces of any paper that can be taped to the chart).

Say something like:

- *When I give you the signal of "Ready, Set, Quest," move around the circle and follow my "commands"—staying linked with your partner. I might say jump, dance, go backward . . . so don't get too crazy and bump into anyone!*

- *While all of you are moving, the Brownie on the left-hand side (raise your hands) gets to tell the Brownie on the right which idea on our Flying into Action Planning Chart she likes best.*

- *When I call "Trade!" all you Brownies on the right fly up to the chart and put your sticky note (paper) on the idea that your partner on the left likes best. Everybody got it?*

Ready, Set, Quest!

Give some silly "Going ELF" commands to let the Brownie energy out as the pairs move around the circle. Consider:

> *Hop on your left feet.*
> *Walk backward.*
> *Walk forward.*
> *Flap your free arms.*
> *Skip.*

In between the silliness, just give a reminder or two like:

- *Brownie on the right, do you know what your partner is voting for? I'm going to call "Trade!" soon.*

BEYOND THIS QUEST

If your Brownie Team will be together beyond this Quest experience and the Team is enthusiastic about many of the ideas, you can let the girls know that you'll save all the ideas in a Brownie Idea Bank, and maybe the Team can do some more of them later in the year or next year.

Ready, Set, Trade

After the Brownies on the right have placed their partner's choices, have the partners switch roles, instructing the Brownies on the left to find out which idea their partners are choosing. Repeat the circle, throwing out some different commands like:

> *March.*
> *Take tiny steps.*
> *Take one step into the circle.*
> *Take two steps out of the circle.*

Ready, Set, Trade Again

After the second set of choices is posted on the chart, have everyone sit (or huddle) to look at the choices.

Get a discussion going, guiding the Brownies to an agreement about their Fly into Action project. You'll want to let the girls know that, because it could be hard to arrange the actual project (because of transportation arrangements, rules related to the place, etc.), you need their top two or three choices—so you can do your best to work out the plans based on their wishes.

Your role in this *cooperative learning exercise*, beyond guiding the girls to an agreement, is to coach the Brownies to give voice to ideas they would like their teammates to consider. You want the girls to understand what it feels like to "compromise" for the Team because they care about each other's ideas.

Discussion prompts might include:

• *Does it look like a lot of you are interested in the same idea? Which one?*

• *How will the girls who chose that idea feel if we don't end up doing it?*

• *Is there any idea that got only a few choices (or none at all) that someone really wanted to try? Would you like to tell the group why you wish that idea had gotten more interest?*

• *How do you think we can make a final decision that our whole Brownie Team will be happy about?*

The outcome of the Team Trade will determine how difficult it might be to come to a group agreement. If the girls seem stuck, propose a few possible solutions—for example, eliminate those projects with the least interest and let the girls choose again (perhaps with a simple show of hands), or keep talking it through to see if any girls change their mind or a new idea emerges.

Brownie Plan: What Information and Supplies Do We Need to Fly into Action?

Now you can move to the last two columns of the Planning Chart by asking the Brownie Team to assist you in really organizing the Fly into Action Project.

For the top choices, ask the girls what they will need to know to take action.

Say something like:

> *OK, so when I contact the _____ (place), what kinds of questions do I need to ask so that we can come in and take action?*

Brainstorm a list of questions or pieces of information the girls want you to find out.

> *What would you like to know about the _____ ?*
>
> *What would help us plan our project?*
>
> *What kinds of things might we need to bring?*

Give the girls some sense of the practical issues involved.

Prompt them with questions like:

> *What if I find out that we can't visit after school (or on weekends)? Should I move to idea number 2?*

Wrap up by letting the girls know that you'll do "your part" to further their plans, and that you'll be letting them know the details. Perhaps you'll be in touch with their families to assist with rides and supplies, etc.

Closing

Today's closing lets the girls reflect on how they selected a project and then decided on ways to take action for it.

Say:

> *You came up with a lot of good ideas today. So now let's write down or share out loud one hope that we have for this project.*

Consider inviting the girls to say the Girl Scout Promise and Law together—after all, they are about to make the world a better place! If you have time, this is a great opportunity to share the Brownie Ballad (page 38 in the girls' book) and ask the girls to describe what they think it means—or even illustrate it!

Tips for Setting Up the Take Action Project

Now that you have ideas about how the Brownie Team would like to Fly into Action, you'll bring the plan to life by using your own skills, the Family and Friends Network, and your knowledge of what is practical and doable.

Reach Out: Share the ideas the girls developed with the Brownie Family and Friends Network and other adult members of your Girl Scout community. Someone may have a connection related to the place where the girls would like to carry out their project and perhaps can put out a few calls or e-mails to get you going.

Inquire: When you make contact with the girls' first-choice place, describe the kind of action the Girl Scout Brownie Team would like to do and why they seem interested in this particular project. Find out what is possible based on the needs of the place. If you can't work out something that is practical and seems to fit the girls' interests, inquire about other similar possibilities the place might suggest. Can't work something out? Don't be discouraged—just move on to the girls' second and third choices. And remember, you may not be able to shape the project exactly as the girls envisioned it. Adjust for reality and let the girls know why you've made some interesting twists to their plan.

Organize: Connect with those members of the Brownie Family and Friends Network who offered to assist, and decide who can do what to support the girls' effort.

Build in Learning by Doing: As you add details to the plan, remember to build in time for the girls to gain new insights about the project—whether about the place they are helping or the people involved there. This expands the Brownies' understanding of "community" and contributes to their knowledge of the community issue and their role in addressing it.

For examples of what might happen as the Brownie Team flies into action, refer to "How the Brownies Might Take Action" on page 73. Of course, the girls may be doing something entirely different that you and they brainstormed about together to make the world a better place!

GIRLS MAKE THE WORLD A BETTER PLACE

Notice the examples of what Girl Scouts and Girl Guides are doing around the world on pages 40-43 in the girls' book. Perhaps they'll spark more ideas for you and the Brownie Team!

PLANTING TREES

Refer back to "The ELF Adventure" story for some inspiration from Campbell, Jamila, and Alejandra. They made a plan for saving a tree family, mostly because they loved the trees and playing around them. As a break from project planning, or as part of reading "The ELF Adventure" story, go outdoors with the girls and play this game:

IF YOU LIVED IN A TREE, WHAT WOULD YOU BE?

- Ask the girls to think of animals they've seen in trees, either in person or on TV or in the movies.

- Have each girl pick her favorite animal and use mime to see if the other girls can guess what her animal is and what it's doing.

- The first girl to guess correctly takes a turn at miming the animal that she chose.

- The girls continue taking turns until each has had a chance to mime her favorite tree-dwelling animal.

Be like elves and do special things,
And be sure to do them well.

—From the Brownie Ballad

SAMPLE SESSIONS 5 & 6
Taking Action and Making the World a Better Place

AT A GLANCE

Goal: The Brownie Team moves forward with its Take Action Project to make an impact in the community and earn its third key.

As the Take Action Project progresses, the Brownies can choose from a range of activities:

- Brownies Get Busy: Depending on their project, the Team creates a skit, gathers supplies or donations, learns about a community issue, etc.

- The Brownie Team Reflects: The girls describe their project and their thoughts about it.

- ELFing It Up: Time permitting, the Team creates "what if" endings to "The ELF Adventure" story, sings Brownie songs, or makes a gift to swap with each other or friends in their wider community.

- Wrapping Up: Brownies conclude their efforts to reach out and make an impact in the community.

- ELFing It Up One More Time: Time permitting, the Team explores new endings or episodes for "The ELF Adventure" story, makes healthy treats, tries the extra puzzles and activities in their Quest books, or creates a closing ceremony.

- Meeting Juliette: The Team considers how Juliette Gordon Low discovered, connected, and took action, and writes to her in their Brownie Quest book.

- Closing Ceremony: Earning the Third Key (Take Action)

The nature of Sessions 5 and 6 will depend on the Brownies' Take Action Project. What follows are simply suggested activities that can be done as the girls engage in their project to maximize the Quest experience.

MATERIALS

- Paper and markers for making mementos and thank-you cards

- Quest Master Map (for display)

- Songs on page 67 of the girls' book (for the Closing Ceremony—make copies as needed)

- Any snacks the girls or the Brownie Network wants for the Closing Ceremony

- Copies of the Take Action Chant (page 91)

Opening Ceremonies

Use the Brownie Circle to give the girls an opportunity to talk about and reflect on the project they are doing.

You might open the circle by saying:

- *We are forming our Brownie Circle today to gather our special skills and strengths and to use them as we Connect and Take Action to make the world a better place.*

- *Let's go around the circle so each of you can say what you hope comes out of the action we're taking.*

Close the reflection by saying the Girl Scout Promise and Law together or singing a Brownie song (see page 67 of the girls' book).

Expanding Their World

Provide the Brownies with opportunities to visit a new place and to interact with new people in the community. Consider a tour of the place their action benefits. Or invite a few special guests related to the project to join the Brownie Circle. Coach the girls to prepare some questions—What do they hope to learn? What are they curious about? Any worries?—so they are ready to talk with the guests.

Memory Keepers

To capture the experience of Flying into Action, have the girls create a memento for their Quest books. They can make a picture of one of the Quest steps and write a few words about it, or they can obtain an information sheet, picture, or brochure from the place their action benefits and attach a scrapbook-style note about the date of their action and what they did.

Mapping the Quest

Be sure to note the points during the sessions when the girls take the second and third steps toward finding the third key, and continue discussing the progress with the Brownies and noting it on the Quest Master Map. (The steps are noted on page 8 and on the Checklist on page 71.)

For example, after the girls have "planned and prepared," you could say:

- *That's the second step to the last key—planning and preparing the Take Action Project! How many steps do we have left? What do you think this key is called?*

UP THE GIRL-LED FACTOR!

Invite the Brownies to create their own opening and closing ceremonies. With your coaching, they can "mix and match," choosing the Brownie Ballad or some Brownie songs, chanting the Brownie cheer (page 94), or making up a cheer of their own!

SAYING THANK YOU

Encourage the Brownies to wrap up their experience by sending thank-you notes to those who assisted with the Take Action Project or other steps along the Quest. Creating a simple expression of thanks lets the girls reflect on what they've learned.

Linking Discover, Connect, and Take Action

As the Brownie Quest is drawing to a close, look for moments to coach the girls on linking the insights they've collected along the way. For example, you could comment on how well they are listening to or supporting each other, reminding them of the Brownie Team Agreement. Or you could make observations about how each Brownie is using some of her special qualities and skills during the Take Action Project. And, of course, there are always opportunities to "catch" girls living the Girl Scout Law!

Closing Ceremony: Earning the Third Key (Take Action)

Regardless of your location or the nature of the girls' project, you'll want to take 10 or 15 minutes at the end of the girls' efforts to form a Brownie Circle. Encourage reflection by asking:

- *How did you act as leaders today, or behind the scenes in preparation for today?*

- *Can you give some examples of choices or decisions you made?*

Encourage cooperation by asking:

- *How are you doing as a Brownie Team and what can you do even better together next time?*

- *What was it like to take action to improve the world? How do you feel about what you accomplished?*

Then say something like:

- *Now we've flown into action and _____(summarize what they have completed—the third step to the third key!).*

- *What were the first two steps? (Identify a problem we care about, and plan an action.)*

- *So the last step is . . . actually doing it.*

- *What do you think the third key is called? (Take Action!)*

- *Now that we have completed the project, we have one more key to add—and a chant to go with it. Here we go! Repeat after me:*

*Flying into action
That's the biggest key!
Improving the world
All around you and me.*

MEETING JULIETTE

Page 72 of the girls' book features a brief biography of Juliette "Daisy" Gordon Low, the founder of Girl Scouts. During Session 5 or 6 give the girls time to think about how Daisy discovered, connected, and took action, as they answer and talk about the reflection questions on page 73 of their book.

SAMPLE SESSION 7: CELEBRATION AND REFLECTION
Unlocking the Code to Leadership

AT A GLANCE

Goal: Depending on the girls' Take Action Project and the time and resources available, the Brownie Team may earn the Take Action Key and "put all the keys together" to earn the Brownie Leadership Quest Award at the close of Session 6. Or you could decide to hold a special Session 7 closing celebration with family and friends.

Either way, allow about 30 minutes for the girls to reflect together on the completion of the Brownie Quest. See pages 68–71 in the girls' book for suggestions.

MATERIALS

- Take Action Keys
- Copies of the full Brownie Quest Chant (page 91)
- Brownie Quest Awards

- Blank index cards and pens
- Optional: The Brownie Ballad or any other Brownie songs, cheers, or stories the Brownies have enjoyed along the Quest.

Time to Put It All Together

Now that the girls have earned their third key, it's time to really see what their keys unlock. In this closing celebration, they will earn their final award—the lock that their keys open. Encourage them to see how their three keys—Discover, Connect, and Take Action—unlock the meaning of leadership.

Encouraging the girls to engage in some reflection really helps bring the leadership journey to full closure. Reflection offers the Brownies the opportunity to "gather" their learning together and internalize it by considering how they might apply it in their lives. Reflection also aids the girls' ability to draw on the Quest experience as they keep on taking action to improve their world.

IF CELEBRATING WITH GUESTS

SET UP DISPLAY STATIONS . . .

. . . featuring key items of the Quest—the Master Map, Brownie Star Circle, Team Agreement, Circle Map, Brainstorm Chart, and something that represents the Take Action Project (perhaps a reply received to the letter they sent to a community official). Divide the Brownies into mini-teams and have each team choose a station to "lead." As guests arrive, the Brownies can show and tell all about their achievements on the Quest.

POST THE WORDS . . .

. . . to the Girl Scout Promise and Law and the Brownie Ballad or other chants, cheers, and songs the Brownies have learned or created along the Quest. Have the Brownies lead their guests in chanting and singing.

SPREAD THE FRIENDSHIP

A giant Friendship Circle (page 27) is a great way to round out the Quest.

Keep the enthusiasm going!

Now's a great time to find out what the Brownies and their families and friends want to do next on the great journey of Girl Scouting!

Earning the Brownie Quest Award and Unlocking the Code to Leadership

Following the Take Action Chant, the Brownies unlock the code of leadership—by thinking about who they are when they put all three keys together. Then they receive the Brownie Quest Award, which is the master lock that requires all three of their keys to open.

BRINGING THE 3 KEYS AND THEIR LOCK TO LIFE

For this last reflection and ceremony, you and the Brownie Family and Friends Network can use your imagination to create a visual prop that conveys the importance of the keys to the girls. Here's one example:

- Draw a giant version of the "lock" that the three keys open on poster boards or cardboard that you can put on the floor or prop up on a table. Or just draw the lock on a large sheet of paper to tape to the wall.

- Make a "master set" of paper or cardboard keys—matching the Discover (star), Connect (circle), and Take Action (wings) keys the Brownies have earned.

As each Brownie gives one example of how she is a leader, invite her to come forward and touch the key to each lock before receiving her Girl Scout Brownie Quest Award.

When you are ready to begin the awards ceremony, say something like:

The Take Action Key is special because it is the last key.

Let's think about what happens when we put the three keys together. Each time you found a key, we had a special chant. Let's put it all together.

Discover Chant

The Discover Key
It's all about me:
What I believe
And my family.

Connect Chant

The Connect Key!
That's more than me.
It's my arms and
your arms.
Linking together,
we're free.

Take Action Chant

Flying into action
That's the biggest key!
Improving the world
All around you and me.

Use the Quest Master Map to prompt the Brownies to give examples related to how they earned the three keys:

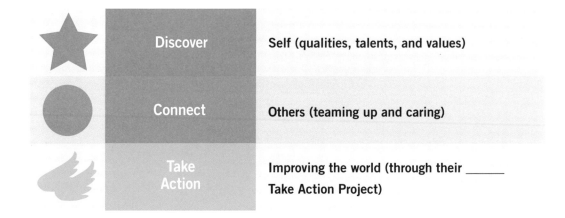

Then say something like:

In Girl Scouts, when a girl Discovers, Connects, and Takes Action, she is showing that she is a leader! Now that you have searched and found the code to leadership—a leader discovers, connects, and takes action—you are a leader!

I'm giving you each a blank card and a pen. Take a few minutes and write a few words or draw a simple picture showing about how you are going to keep on being a leader in your life. (If family and friends are attending the closing, invite them to assist their Brownies.)

Give the girls a few minutes and then say:

Let's go around our circle one last time, and each one of you can say one way that you are going to keep on being a leader!

After each Brownie gives her "leadership commitment," award her the Brownie Quest Award. Then, remind all the Brownies that they can now use their keys to open this master lock—and to keep on opening doors to more leadership adventures in Girl Scouting!

Cheers and a Big Send-Off

Close the Quest with the Girl Scout Promise and Law and any songs, skits, cheers, or chants the girls have made up or enjoyed along the way. Invite the girls to add some last memory keepers to their Brownie Quest books, including their "leadership card" autographs from family and friends, or the complete chant or cheer (provided at the end of this section for you to copy).

Then say to the girls something like:

• *Now that you have your three keys to lead, you can use them to keep on opening doors to more leadership adventures in Girl Scouting.*

Encourage them to go off and spend some more time "getting to know" Girl Scout founder Juliette "Daisy" Gordon Low (page 72 in their books). Let them know that Daisy was a leader who can inspire them for the rest of their lives.

Brownie Cheer

Here's a little riddle
To end the Brownie Quest:

We may not be all that old
But we're not so little that we fold.

We don't have keys to the family car
Or even a locker in the school hall,
But we Brownies still know how to rule:

With ELF on our side,
We Discover, Connect, and
Take Action high and wide.

So can you guess what we are?

Leaders—all of us, every one!

So watch out, world,
Here we come.
We're Girl Scout Brownies,
And we get the job done!

And now, congratulations to you!
Turn back to the reflection on leadership
(page 34) and think about
what you have learned and
accomplished along the
Quest with the Brownies!

Three cheers for you!